W9-ANM-577

NEW ZEALAND JOURNEY

NEW ZEALAND JOURNEY

VERENA & GEORG POPP

craig potton publishing

First published in 2008 by Craig Potton Publishing
Reprinted 2011

Craig Potton Publishing
98 Vickerman Street, PO Box 555, Nelson, New Zealand
www.craigpotton.co.nz

Reprinted 2009

Photography © Verena & Georg Popp

ISBN 978 1 877333 92 7

Printed in China by Midas Printing International Ltd

This book is copyright. Apart from any fair dealing for the purposes of private study,
research, criticism or review, as permitted under the Copyright Act, no part may be
reproduced by any process without the permission of the publishers.

Opposite Rock platform, Kaikoura Peninsula

Sunset on Mt Taranaki from the Pouakai Tarns, Egmont National Park

Preface

VISITING NEW ZEALAND for the first time a few years ago was a truly special occasion for us. Not only had we been dreaming for a long time of going to this country on the other side of the planet but, most of all, it was so special because it was our first overseas trip with our seven-month-old daughter Stella. It was, we thought, a good time to go on a photography trip without any assignments, deadlines or schedules. The big unanswered question was whether we could manage to balance the professional landscape photographer's life of travel and business obligations with family affairs, and still make everyone involved happy.

Long before our arrival we knew that New Zealand is unarguably a landscape photographer's paradise – just thumbing through the pages of travel guides revealed images of glaciers, high alpine peaks, rainforests, meadows, volcanoes, deserts, fiords, rugged shorelines and subtropical beaches, all jammed into a country the size of Germany. Trading the cold and wet winter of Vienna for summer and strolls along unspoiled beaches didn't seem to be such a bad deal either!

What we didn't quite realise back then was how many great photographers there were in New Zealand, who had covered in spectacular ways so much of what there was to see. It was the time before *The Lord of the Rings*, and so New Zealand was neither such a widespread subject in magazines and on bookshelves, nor did we, in the middle of Europe, hear much about its photographers. To see the high standard of landscape photographs was a surprise. We bought Andris Apse's book *New Zealand Landscapes* and Craig Potton's *Moment and Memory* right away at Auckland International Airport, even before stepping out of the terminal. For us, looking at inspiring photographs and paintings has always been important when trying to improve our own ways of seeing and to expand our creative vision. In this case, however, we also felt a little bit intimidated. Many of the most breathtaking images were taken on far-flung places like Campbell Island, Auckland

Island or inaccessible spots on the main islands. Others, taken in more accessible regions, featured rather special occasions, like the eruption of Mt Ruapehu, the Canterbury pastures or Central Otago highlands freshly dusted with snow, or extreme storms that blew away whole waterfalls in Fiordland National Park. Yes, there is something like a home-court advantage in nature photography.

These were images we would have loved to produce ourselves but we knew that we were not even going to come close, no matter how hard we tried. Furthermore, having decided to take our first child along on our journey, we wondered if we could come up with the high photographic standard that we always set for ourselves. The best solution for the time being seemed to be to just drift along, get a feeling for the country and let the images come to us, instead of trying to force them. And in the many weeks that followed on that first trip, that is what we did: we let little Stella set the pace and when she was happy, we were too. Not only did we enjoy our time in New Zealand, living like vagabonds in our motor home, but, much to our surprise, we came away with an astoundingly high rate of 'keepers' – images we were very happy with. Besides being published in several magazines, some of them were printed in a large wall calendar that received a gold medal for Best Scenic Calendar from the Calendar Marketing Association in the USA, and an image of the Moeraki Boulders in sweet morning light (see page 79) earned us first place in the prestigious *Euro Press* photo competition. We could never have guessed that one journey, which held so many doubts, would help us to plant a firm foot in the photography business.

One year later our family grew to four as our second daughter Livia was born, and we decided New Zealand would again be the best place to see whether travelling and photographing with two little children would work out. It did indeed work out – perfectly – and we came back again and again and again. New Zealand became something of a second home to us and we reserved at least one journey each year, lasting several months. Our daughters now surprise their teachers when, instead of knowing the most recent cartoon series on TV, they tell them what a pukeko is, or a kiwi, kakapo or kea – or, of course, a sandfly! They have seen albatrosses, sea lions, seals and glowworms from close up, and regard it as the most normal thing on earth.

We still like to view all the images from the books we bought on our first trip, but they are no longer intimidating. We know we have found our own way of seeing New Zealand, and so many more photo opportunities were made possible because of the slow and unrushed, even unadventurous, way we travelled with our kids, rather than racing from one classic icon shot to the next, trying to cover it all in a rush. Our favourite images show rather ordinary places where we just happened to be when the light was right. The weather and light conditions in New Zealand are continually changing, and that convinced us to spend extra days at those places we liked very much, and to look very carefully for the heart of the place, the essence so to speak.

We never intended to cover all of the country with our photography, but instead to enjoy being there as much as we could and transport that feeling into the images. This book is not so much a planned project as a collection of many single moments, each one memorable to us. Looking at the images that we put together for this book, we found that nearly all of them were taken in places that can be easily visited. Part of the reason for publishing this book was that we thought it might be an inspiration for others to visit those places and see for themselves. If you do so, we would urge you not just to go there but to slow down, to stay for a while. Listen to the sounds, watch the light change and feel the wind or rain. Pick up an empty shell or admire the incredible diversity of driftwood. Look at all those little things you can find, just as children love to. This can be just as memorable as some of the more famous views.

Besides the photography experience, it has been the slow pace of life, and the ability to seize each given moment and to be open to things happening to us, instead of rushing and forcing our luck, that has had the most lasting effect on us. Our New Zealand journeys have not only made us much better photographers but have vastly improved our lives and we will always feel extremely grateful for that.

Verena & Georg Popp
Vienna, June 2008

Morning light on the Moeraki Boulders, Otago

Photographers' Notes

Nearly all the landscape images in this book were taken with a 4 x 5" large format camera and equipment. (The only exceptions are the photos on pages 126 and 127.) Nature photography with this type of camera, probably far off the beaten track or roadside, is quite painstaking, tiresome, complicated, old-fashioned and rather costly. Modern field cameras, like the ones we prefer to use, don't differ much from the models that William H. Jackson used more than 100 years ago to take the first images of what would later become Yellowstone National Park. Everything still functions manually, neither zoom lenses nor autofocus are available, and our headlamps and hand-held spot meter (for determining the exposure) are the only battery-driven devices to be found in our backpacks. Large-format landscape photography is also still largely analogue, which means using film. Not that we large-format photographers are such sentimental people that we despise everything digital, nor do we necessarily love film over everything else, but there is simply no practicable alternative. The main goal is to get the highest possible print quality, no matter the size of the reproduction, and at the same time to have sturdy equipment that is reliable to work with even under the sometimes rough conditions out in the wilderness. Current 'pixel-giants' like Hasselblad's H3D can't offer the crucial versatile movements of view cameras, and digital scanning backs (such as those from Phase One which can be used with large-format cameras), are not yet an option. You would be unlikely to take a fragile, $50,000 (at least) camera set-up that is very dependent on electricity and vulnerable to dust and water, on a two-week sea kayak trip through rainy Doubtful Sound, or on a hike through the wind-blown sand dunes of Te Paki Reserve.

If you want to put captivating images onto a 4 x 5" (10.2 x 12.7 cm) sheet of film, there are hardly any technical developments that make it an easy endeavour. Does this mean one must be crazy or masochistic to use large format? Of course not, but there are some very obvious reasons, and some less obvious ones, to do so.

The many movements of a view camera (to correct perspectives, or to focus from front to back, for example) are some of the very obvious features in comparison to an SLR or medium-format camera. But it is the large film size – 4 x 5" film is approximately 15 times larger than a 35 mm slide or four times larger than 6 x 6 cm film – that is the main reason many people try their luck with it. The advantage of the size is that it delivers an impressive crispness and clarity, especially in larger print sizes, that cannot be achieved otherwise.

On the one hand this is a very legitimate reason for using large format, but it also means we have to know our gear very well and be able to use it quickly. The fast-changing light and weather conditions in New Zealand often put all our experience to the test. We didn't always react and work quickly enough, and these were the moments when we wished for digital alternatives!

On the other hand, when the skies were overcast or the weather stable, it meant we had to work even harder to come away with new and fresh compositions, which are more than just simple documents in colour. No other type of camera gives you more control over composing an image than a large-format view camera. But there is a steep learning curve

involved, and it is extremely important to not be overwhelmed by the sheer amount of gear needed or the difficult handling of a view camera, because it could result in an over-conservative style that can quickly become banal or even boring. Even physical fitness plays a key role in our work, as it would be frustrating to reach a mountaintop in the best possible light only to be so out of breath that you can't think straight and miss the opportunity. We carry our backpacks of 25 kilograms or more over mountains, through forests and deserts, or by sea kayak on the ocean – sometimes for one day, sometimes for two weeks on end. But the one thing that we always try to ensure is that the technical aspect of using large format does not dictate the emotional message of an image.

Many of the advantages of large-format photography will only become apparent after you have been using it for some time. Experience will make many things easier after a while, and the more you get used to composing and focusing an image upside down and backwards on the viewing glass, the more you can concentrate on the creative process. The awkwardness of large format forces you to work extremely carefully. You might work as carefully with other equipment too, but with large format it

Beech forest in mist near Green Lake, Fiordland National Park

Morning mist over Lake Matheson, Westland/Tai Poutini National Park

is mandatory. As a logical consequence, we expose only about 2000 sheets of film each·year. A certain percentage goes straight to the rubbish bin, and a number of transparencies will be used for back-ups or to experiment with exposures, so we usually end up with not much more than 100 totally different images each year. Of these 100, only 10 or 12 are good enough to really excite us and to be included in an exhibition. (This is usually the highest criterion for us, when judging a transparency on the light table.) It is a very modest number of photos, but we have learned to use it to our advantage. Knowing we do not need a large number of images to make a living from them, we never feel rushed while on a photography trip and take our time to stay and wait that extra day, or even a week, until the light is just right.

Another advantage is revealed after coming back from such a journey. On a large light table we spread out the transparencies and quickly get an overview of which are the bad ones, which are the keepers and which the are highlights. It's only a matter of hours. No thumbing through thousands of digital files or 35 mm slides for days on end. After two days all the images are scanned and filed away, leaving us time to think about future projects or the business work, which we actually do enjoy quite a lot, as it gives us a needed contrast to the long periods spent outdoors far from any comforts. After 10 years of professional landscape photography we can say that our job has become a greater hobby than it was at the beginning. Landscape photography has become something of a lifestyle, like a path to follow, but also one that gives us the freedom to create our own personal trekking tour through life.

The seemingly obvious simplicity of photographing landscapes, because they do not shake or hide or run away, is one of the hardest challenges of all to overcome. For us it is not enough to just find the right exposure and focus, as it might be when taking pictures of a rare and shy bird. Simple documentation in landscape photography is a thing of the past and, in a world full of visual overload, it takes some effort to keep the viewer's attention for more than a fleeting second. It is that extra time taken when a photo draws your eyes, evokes your emotions, or just makes you curious, which matters the most to us.

Verena & Georg Popp

Rock formation near Totaranui Beach at sunset, Abel Tasman National Park

Totaranui Beach, Abel Tasman National Park

Sand dunes at Wharariki Beach, Golden Bay

Sunset at Wharariki Beach, Golden Bay

Scotts Beach and Kohaihai Bluff at sunset, Kahurangi National Park

Boulders on the coastal section of the Heaphy Track, Kahurangi National Park

Nikau palms along the Heaphy Track, Kahurangi National Park

Kohaihai River, at the start of the Heaphy Track, Kahurangi National Park

Boulder beach on the Heaphy Track, Kahurangi National Park

Evening light at the Kohaihai River mouth, Kahurangi National Park

Ferns and young rimu in the Oparara Basin, Kahurangi National Park

Blechnum ferns growing beside the Oparara River, Kahurangi National Park

Inside Moria Gate, a limestone arch in the Oparara Basin, Kahurangi National Park

The Oparara River flowing through Moria Gate, Kahurangi National Park

Rocks in the Fox River valley, Paparoa National Park

A fruiting nikau palm on the Paparoa coastline, Paparoa National Park

West Coast beaches north of Punakaiki, Paparoa National Park

Coastal forest on the ridges of Paparoa National Park

The Pancake Rocks at Dolomite Point, Paparoa National Park

Coastal rocks near Haast, South Westland

The terminal face of Franz Josef Glacier, Westland/Tai Poutini National Park

Algae and lichen encrust rocks in the Waiho Valley,
Westland/Tai Poutini National Park

A white heron, or kotuku, nesting in the Waitangiroto Nature Reserve,
South Westland

Mt Tasman and Aoraki/Mt Cook reflected in Lake Matheson, Westland/Tai Poutini National Park

Three Mile Lagoon, South Westland

Native sand-binding grass growing on Gillespies Beach, South Westland

Franz Josef Glacier from Sentinel Rock, Westland/Tai Poutini National Park

Lake Matheson, Westland/Tai Poutini National Park

Driftwood on the beach at Bruce Bay, South Westland

Rimu trees line the shore at Bruce Bay, South Westland

Eroded limestone rocks near Monro Beach, South Westland

Water-worn boulders cover the beach at Bruce Bay, South Westland

Rainforest near Haast, South Westland

Kahikatea forest growing in swampland near Ship Creek, South Westland

Fiordland crested penguin on Monro Beach, South Westland

Evening light at Haast Beach, South Westland

Coastal cliffs near Knights Point, South Westland

Rimu tree in coastal forest, South Westland

Rocky gorge by the Haast River, Mount Aspiring National Park

Flowering rata near Haast Pass, Mount Aspiring National Park

Tussock and mountain beech near Borland Pass, Fiordland National Park

Key Summit on the Routeburn Track, Fiordland National Park

Summer flowers in Milford Sound, Fiordland National Park

Sunrise on Mitre Peak in Milford Sound, Fiordland National Park

Pingao growing on sand dunes at Mason Bay, Rakiura National Park, Stewart Island

Flax and rushes, Mason Bay, Rakiura National Park, Stewart Island

Sand dunes and pingao at Mason Bay, Rakiura National Park, Stewart Island

Looking north from Mason Bay, Rakiura National Park, Stewart Island

Coastal shrubland and sand dunes meet at Mason Bay, Rakiura National Park, Stewart Island

Wind-shorn coastal shrubland, Mason Bay, Rakiura National Park, Stewart Island

The North Catlins coast near Kaka Point, with Nugget Point lighthouse visible, Otago

Nugget Point on the North Catlins coast, Otago

Stream near McLean Falls in Catlins Forest Park, Otago

The Catlins River, Catlins Forest Park, Otago

McLean Falls on the Tautuku River, Catlins Forest Park, Otago

Lake Wilkie, Catlins Forest Park, Otago

Drowned trees at Pounawea, The Catlins, Otago

Sunset at Curio Bay, South Catlins, Southland

Kelp at low tide in Curio Bay, South Catlins, Southland

Tidal rock platforms in Curio Bay, South Catlins, Southland

Allans Beach and Hoopers Inlet, Otago Peninsula

New Zealand or Hooker's sea lion, Surat Bay, Otago

The Moeraki Boulders, Otago

Morning light on the Moeraki Boulders, Otago

Lake Wanaka viewed from Roys Peak, Otago

Eastern shore of Lake Pukaki, Mackenzie Country

Aoraki/Mt Cook above the Mueller and Hooker glaciers, Aoraki/Mount Cook National Park

Mount Cook buttercup and *Celmisia*, Hooker Valley,
Aoraki/Mount Cook National Park

Kea, Aoraki/Mount Cook National Park

The South Face of Aoraki/Mt Cook, Aoraki/Mount Cook National Park

The Devil's Punchbowl Falls, Arthur's Pass National Park

The braided gravel riverbed of the Waimakariri River, Arthur's Pass National Park

The Seaward Kaikoura Range from the Kaikoura Peninsula

Kaitorete Spit at Birdlings Flat, Canterbury

New Zealand fur seal, Kaikoura, Marlborough

New Zealand fur seal, Kaikoura, Marlborough

A royal albatross, or toroa, Otago Peninsula

Rock platforms on the Kaikoura Peninsula, Marlborough

Alpine tarn near Lewis Pass, North Canterbury

Lichen-covered beech forest near Lewis Pass, North Canterbury

Mt Stokes, above the Marlborough Sounds

View of the Marlborough Sounds from Mt Stokes

Castlepoint lighthouse, Wairarapa

Sunset at Cape Palliser, Wairarapa

Cape Kidnappers, Hawke's Bay

Australasian gannet colony at Cape Kidnappers, Hawke's Bay

Mt Taranaki from the Pouakai Range, Egmont National Park

Mt Taranaki reflected in a tarn on the Pouakai Range, Egmont National Park

Subalpine forest, Egmont National Park

Mt Taranaki from The Plateau, Egmont National Park

Introduced heather on the approach to Mt Ngauruhoe, Tongariro National Park

Blue Lake on Mt Tongariro, Tongariro National Park

Volcanic landforms on the Tongariro Crossing, Tongariro National Park

The Emerald Lakes on Mt Tongariro, Tongariro National Park

Alpine plants beside Blue Lake, Mt Tongariro, Tongariro National Park

Alpine plants, Tongariro National Park

Red Crater and Mt Ngauruhoe, Tongariro National Park

Tree Trunk Gorge in Kaimanawa Forest Park, Central North Island

Bridal Veil Falls, Raglan, Waikato

Lake Taupo at Awaroa Reserve, Central North Island

Te Whaiti Nui A Toi Canyon in Whirinaki Forest Park, Central North Island

Kahikatea forest beside Arahaki Lagoon, Whirinaki Forest Park, Central North Island

Tree ferns, or punga, in Te Urewera National Park

Korokoro Falls, Te Urewera National Park

Waimangu Volcanic Valley, Rotorua

Whakarewarewa Thermal Valley, Rotorua

The Marble Terrace in Waimangu Volcanic Valley, Rotorua

Champagne Pool in Waiotapu Thermal Reserve, Rotorua

Volcanic activity on White Island, Bay of Plenty

Crater lake on White Island, Bay of Plenty

Rainbow over a headland on the Coromandel Peninsula

Evening light off the Coromandel coast

Tane Mahuta, New Zealand's largest kauri tree,
in Waipoua Forest, Northland

Spirits Bay, Cape Reinga, Northland

Beach in Matai Bay, Karikari Peninsula, Northland

Shell-strewn beach on Karikari Peninsula, Northland

Pohutukawa tree, Karikari Peninsula, Northland

Matai Bay on Karikari Peninsula, Northland

Sand dunes in Te Paki Recreation Reserve, Northland

Ninety Mile Beach, Northland

Beach on Karikari Peninsula, Northland

Flax in a lagoon on Karikari Peninsula, Northland

View northwards from Cape Reinga, Northland

Cape Reinga lighthouse, Northland

Last light on Mt Stokes and the Marlborough Sounds